How To Be Funny

A Guide to Developing Your Sense of Humour and Funny Comment Delivery to Lighten the Mood and Make People Laugh

by Raj Farkas

Table of Contents

Introduction 1

Chapter 1: Basic Rules of Humour 7

Chapter 2: How to Physically Loosen Up for Humour 15

Chapter 3: How to Mentally Loosen Up for Humour 21

Chapter 4: Some Important Points in Humour 29

Chapter 5: Other Practices to Boost Comic Delivery 37

Conclusion 41

Introduction

President Obama walks up on stage and gravely begins with *"I'm here to announce, that we're building Iron Man."* Boom! Instant comedy! Now, politics aside, there's a guy who knows how to lighten the mood like a ***boss***!

Not surprisingly, social skills are held in the highest regard nowadays. Among them, the ability to be funny is one of the most cherished. Why? Because it gives you the ability to read a room and orchestrate the emotions of people in it like a pro. Now, if any of you just went (wait, let me quickly put on geek glasses and a pocket protector. For best effects read as a whiny voice QQing), "But, work quality also counts. Grades matter. I'm a genius." (cue sarcasm) Yeah, that's precisely why you're reading this guide right now.

Here's a little tip – life ***is*** a popularity contest, and being charming is strongly equated with being witty and funny. Moreover, the higher up on the ladder you stand, the more people love you for being self-deprecating. A PR-competent CEO at a press conference needs to know how to throw a custard pie of humility on his own face with one hand, while simultaneously conducting the sonata of his organization with his other, and also avoiding the banana peels laid down by the press while replacing them with his own for comic effect. People love those who make them laugh — and the more surprising the source, the better (all you tax collectors and insurance salesmen out there, here's your chance).

Although they say humour is something a person's either born with or completely lacks, that's not altogether true. The essentials of humour can be learned, especially if you're willing to develop a quick wit and practice your timing. Quick! What's an addict's favorite online encyclopedia? Give up? I'll give the answer in the chapters to come. We definitely need to re-activate your funny bone.

And *that's* why you're here. Because although you may not have been blessed with the most natural sense of humour, it *can* be inculcated. There are various basic principles and mentalities involved which, when learned, can turn even the driest of humour impaired people (yes, I'm looking at you!) into a regular stand-up comic. Get it? This guide isn't here to teach you 101 jokes about the clown, the rabbi and the zucchini who walked into a bar — it's here to *make* **you** genuinely funny! So, without wasting any more time, let's get started!

© Copyright 2015 by Miafn LLC - All rights reserved.

This document is geared towards providing reliable information in regards to the topic and issue covered. The publication is sold with the idea that the publisher is not required to render accounting, officially permitted, or otherwise, qualified services. If advice is necessary, legal or professional, a practiced individual in the profession should be ordered.

- From a Declaration of Principles which was accepted and approved equally by a Committee of the American Bar Association and a Committee of Publishers and Associations.

In no way is it legal to reproduce, duplicate, or transmit any part of this document in either electronic means or in printed format. Recording of this publication is strictly prohibited and any storage of this document is not allowed unless with written permission from the publisher. All rights reserved.

The information provided herein is stated to be truthful and consistent, in that any liability, in terms of inattention or otherwise, by any usage or abuse of any policies, processes, or directions contained within is solely and completely the responsibility of the recipient reader. Under no circumstances will any legal responsibility or blame be held against the publisher for any reparation, damages, or monetary loss due to the information herein, either directly or indirectly.

Respective authors own all copyrights not held by the publisher.

The information herein is offered for informational purposes solely, and is universal as so. The presentation of the information is without contract or any type of guarantee assurance.

The trademarks that are used are without any consent, and the publication of the trademark is without permission or backing by the trademark owner. All trademarks and brands within this book are for clarifying purposes only and are the owned by the owners themselves, not affiliated with this document.

Chapter 1: Basic Rules of Humour

As you get lost in the depths of this eldritch grimoire, its power and bedazzling potential dragging you deeper into its untapped mysteries, a creepy old man in a dusty robe, with a single tooth and a unibrow more magnificent than Nicholas Cage's, pops up behind you and drops a User Manual on your head (fine, *Mystic* user manual. Happy?)

"Apprentiſe, here thou ſhalt learn the baſic ruleſ of humour. If thou veer from theſe here lawſ, may the fleaſ of a thouſand camelſ infeſt your armpitſ." *Whoosh Pop.*

Rule 1: Always Make Fun of Yourself

Now this seems a bit counter-productive to most people. They want to become funnier to be better liked or better equipped for social encounters, and as it is if you need help being funny – chances are people made enough fun of you while growing up. But, here's the genius of this – if you beat people to the punch-line, they'll lose interest in making fun of you. So, the fastest way to being respected in social circles is to be jovial and self-deprecating. Always take an insult with a smile, and never waste a chance to turn it into a joke. Take Abraham Lincoln as an example. This late great President was often a humble man and was quite aware that his face was probably one that only a mother could truly love. In one of their debates, Senator Stephen Douglas once accused Lincoln of being two-faced, implying Lincoln's overt homeliness to be a farce. To this, Honest Abe coolly responded: "If I were two-faced, would I be wearing this one?"

Humour directed at yourself will always make you more approachable and likable. It will also boost your self-esteem and give you the confidence of an Alpha. Never miss an opportunity to pull your own leg for the amusement of others.

Rule 2: Don't Use Humour as a Weapon

While stand-up comedians use plenty of insult comedy to great effect, it won't work out quite as well for you if you do the same in daily conversations. If you truly want to use some insult comedy, it should come after a solid 10 minutes of making fun of yourself and getting people to laugh at you first. It establishes that your intentions aren't to insult someone, but rather to make everyone laugh. It also makes you more likable if you manage to be funny without hurting someone else's feelings for it. Of course, if you're that close to someone that you know what their threshold between funny and offensive is, go for it as a friendly ribbing from time to time. If you want to break this rule in general public, be prepared to receive the tender love and adulation of your audience flying towards your face as well.

Hazing someone else for the sake of making people laugh is *never* funny, and neither are puns.

Rule 3: Play Your Own Strengths

Once you figure out what your brand of humour is, don't imitate someone else's just because you saw it get more laughs. Humour should magnify your own personality, not turn you into a second-rate copy of someone else. While you could definitely use jokes and one-liners from others in your own repertoire, don't try and mimic their styles. The personality needed to successfully deliver some jokes may not match your own.

Rule 4: Never Laugh at Your Own Joke

It's sad, pathetic, needy, the list of adjectives is unending. You *should* keep on smiling, but don't crack up at your own humour right after delivering a punch-line. Not only will that turn people off of your comedic sense fast, you'll also lose their respect. The corollary to this is: Always laugh harder at other people's jokes than your own. If you don't want to do that, develop a chuckle for all occasions.

Rule 5: Avoid Stereotyping

Stay away from overtly profane, sexist or sexual jokes unless you're absolutely sure your audience will receive them well. As a safe bet, stay away from them in professional settings altogether. Also, jokes are funny when people aren't made to feel bad about themselves, or when they're not being negatively stereotyped. With that in mind, avoid racist and ageist jokes. If you wish to poke fun at someone, use observational humour to make the joke about *them* and not about a stereotypical pigeonhole in which you're putting them. Keep in mind that if you want to keep a joke humourous and personal, it should ideally have an insult and a compliment in the same sentence – or preferably even an insult to yourself and a compliment to them. E.g. If you want to harmlessly poke fun at a friend who's quite obsessive about her work and yet is faster than you or works harder than you - *"I go through a book so slowly, Sandy must feel like the OCD Flash when reading beside me."* Always keep in mind that if you personally call out someone whom you don't know well enough, even friendly ribbing can backfire horribly.

Rule 6: Always Know Your Audience

Every individual has a slightly different comedic sensibility than when they're in a group. In group dynamics, one or two people chuckling usually gets the others laughing as well. If the power relationship in the dynamic is slightly skewed, i.e. there's a boss woman or boss man in the circle, the funniest humour for the group is usually dictated by the tastes of the leader. If you're entering a new social circle that seems to obviously have a dominant personality, crack jokes that they will appreciate the most to get the strongest responses from the group as a whole.

Besides using your knowledge to manipulate a group, there are also settings and circumstances under which the entire mentality of a group may be quite different – if a particularly vicious group loves ageist jokes within themselves, chances are even they won't find such humour funny at a funeral. Always be aware of your surroundings, and if you're on a roll – don't get carried away into blurting out something stupid.

Chapter 2: How to Physically Loosen up for Humour

Yes, you read the title right. Humour is just as strongly about body language as it is about the actual words. In fact, most comedians might say it's much more important. Picture Russell Peters' jokes coming out of the mouth of a small, scrawny dude with bad posture – and no, I'm not talking about Aziz Ansari. *Heyo!* Nah, I kid. That guy has impeccable body language.

I mean imagine the same jokes being repeated by someone with bad posture and a shy voice that's struggling to be heard. Not quite the same, is it?

So, if you want to become funnier, the first thing you need to do is change the message which your body sends out from a sort of * pssh * to a more * BOOM pffft *, if you know what I mean (If you do, you're a bloody genius).

The biggest change that needs to happen is in your facial area. If you're not used to smiling a lot, and you try and change that right away – you're going to come across as creepy because your muscles *literally* won't be used to holding that expression. So, your first piece of homework is to go in front of a mirror and give me a hundred smiles. Stat! Hop to it, soldier! You'll notice your smile becoming a bit tense and droopy around the 30-mark. Work on your smile, and adjust it, till you find one that says "I love making fun of myself, and I take nothing seriously... but there's some deeper mystery in me as well" (So, no. No Heath Ledger-Joker grin). If a straight smile with lots of teeth doesn't work for you, try a crooked one – works wonders for me, if you know what I mean. But the nuance of a smile means that your crooked smile should be dashing, not rapey – and believe you me, it's a fine line.

Once you've landed on a smile that works for you, get to work on your body language. People who need help becoming funnier usually have one thing in common – they take themselves far too seriously. This shows in the stiff way they walk or the unchanging set of their shoulders. Whether or not they're confident of themselves in other social aspects, they come across as miserable.

Did you know that your body language can *induce* joy and happiness in you just as strongly as your mood affects your body language? This means that if you set your body to show that you're happy, your mind will feel lighter and happier as well!

With that in mind, work on loosening your body. Stand in front of a mirror (or not. It's not compulsory), and just loosen the muscles in your body. Don't tense anything or concentrate too hard on holding yourself straight. Once you're loosened up, hunch and give me ten Igors! Lower your head and shoulders till you get a hunch on your back, bend your knees and loosen your arms – move like a monkey with arms flailing intoning "Yeth, Mathter" ten times.

While this may be silly, that's *precisely* the point. It's to be a little silly and to get you out of your own head. If you enjoy it, you could also bust out this move if someone's being a little bossy and you want to make the people around you crack up. This is a perfect example of witty physical humour without acting like a clown.

When you're outside, your body language should show that you're confident without being too deeply set within yourself. Keep your shoulders straight and back, but without seeming to be rigid for it. Keep your arms a little loose, and not like a soldier's during a march. Keep your strides measured and long, not short, but without looking like a robot. This should give you a confident swagger. The rest also depends on the setting and your clothing.

If you're in a professional setting, your body language *should* reflect a confident, business personality. However, in such settings, your smile and words will do most of the lightening up for you.

When you're in more relaxed settings, change up your clothing to include some brighter colored apparel – if you don't have any. Chances are that if you're a little humour impaired, you like to stick to safer or duller colors like some shades of brown, blue, gray, green, black or white. Experiment outside your comfort zone to see which other colors may fit you well. A sunny disposition makes all the difference when you're in a social group. If your clothes make you look like the dark cloud on the horizon, all your other efforts will only get you a polite chuckle at most.

No matter what setting you're in, or whichever situation you may be faced with (again, unless it's a funeral), have a million-watt smile on. Now that you've figured out and practiced the smile that works best for you, bust it out as often as you can. Since you want to make people laugh, the easiest way to induce an atmosphere of humour is to always be happy and upbeat yourself.

Chapter 3: How to Mentally Loosen up for Humour

If you have the personality of a wet blanket, you can't hope to bring sunshine and smiles in other people's lives. As I've mentioned before, humour can't truly be learnt for best effect – it's something that has to come up from deep inside you. Therefore, you need to alter your mental wavelength a bit to make yourself funnier. For all you granite-faced tax collectors and Men In Black out there, don't worry – this won't hurt, much.

Tip 1: Dive Headlong into Funny Stuff

Most people who *aren't* funny, think that they'll get time in a conversation to think, analyze and deliver the perfect joke from their eidetic compilation of memorized joke-books. The truth, you poor lost souls, is that conversational humour is more a product of instantaneous wit than of preparation. It rises out of your subconscious and is funny because it's the perfect thing to apply to the situation and can be said in a short amount of time. If someone does something funny, and it takes you three minutes to come up with a humourous response – all you'll hear in appreciation are the crickets in the background.

Therefore, stop watching your super-serious documentaries and start watching funny stuff instead (Put that stand-up origin documentary down, or so help me God). Immerse yourself in the work of comedic genii and dive headlong into shows like F.R.I.E.N.D.S which have become the backbone of pop culture comedy. Find stand-up comedians whose style matches your own comedic sensibilities and bury yourself in their work. Give those tired self-help books (this one's an exception, obviously) a break, and get humourous non-fiction novels instead. The more deeply you surround yourself with funny works – audio-visual or textual – the faster you'll find yourself thinking of humourous responses when situations arise. This will also give you a great sense of what your own style of humour is like.

Once you've started developing your own sense of humour, it's acceptable to start trawling websites and books for funny one-liners, jokes and witty quips which fit your sense of humour. They're only acceptable as resources to *enhance* your own sense of humour, and not to replace it. Such sources give you funny fodder to memorize which you could use at an appropriate moment.

Tip 2: Get Used to Saying Random Funny Stuff

Everyday life gives up plenty of opportunities that we miss out on, simply because we're not creative enough to come up with a funny way of exploiting them.

In the spirit of this revelation, let me give you a small golden nugget that you can bring out at any moment to make people laugh. Start busting out over-dramatic, nonsensical, asinine reactions.

One common thing that happens to most of us is that people either come up to gossip, or to reveal something small and mundane, etc. - basically to chat. When someone tells you a bit of news, throw our random reactions. Instead of throwing out bored, dull responses like "Uhuh" or "Mmhmm" or "Okay" or "Go on" or "Wow", and instead exclaim the following:

"Sweet Tomatoes of Kackerfrazzle!"

"Sweet Kumquat of Bougainvillea!"

Or some other like brilliance. You get the point.

This is the easiest way of lightening the mood and making people laugh. And all it really needs from you is to string together nonsensical random words in a sentence and say them in an exclamatory fashion. How could I **possibly** spoon-feed you more?

Tip 3: Respect the Inner Workings of Humour

Everything apart from fart jokes and puns has an elegant mechanic of its own. Now, most of you must be wondering why I hate puns in humour. The simple answer is – it comes off as trying too hard. Puns and word-play are funny in textual humour, to a point, but not in conversational humour. This is simply because they mostly depend on homophones – words that sound similar but may be different in spelling and meaning. But, the problem is that if I'm talking to you right now, you brain places each word in the sentence in context with the meaning you think I'm trying to put across. E.g. If I say to you "Damn, that's a beautiful flower", your mind will automatically fill in "flower" and not "flour", simply because that's what makes sense in the context of the sentence. Similarly, it won't replace "flour" with "flower" if I say "This bread's made from the highest-quality whole-wheat flour". Usually, the only one who cracks up after a pun is the person who made the joke – and maybe one other dork who's freakishly in sync with their wavelength. More often, you'll have to explain the pun you just made, and nothing kills a joke faster.

Most humour comes from surprise, expectation, observation and misdirection. The examples I gave in the previous tip are funny because they come as a surprise and they're not what someone would normally expect as an exclamation in a normal conversation. There are easy ways to implement this in everyday conversations without having to set up a joke and deliver a punch-line. If a close friend is famously anti-religious for example and asks you "Know what I heard today?" you could fake-excitedly reply with "A prayer?". Or, if you've been to a party the previous evening, and meet up with a friend from there the next evening after work, you could ask: "Know how my day went?" and when he answers with the invariable "How?" -you go: "I don't remember. That's why I'm asking You!"

The point is to play on normal expectations. If you deliver something that shifts away from the expected, or blow it completely out of the water, you'll get a laugh.

You could even delve into classics to get a laugh in an appropriate setting. For example, if you're drinking with friends of your own gender and you're close enough to tolerate a few boundary issues – Throw out a super-dramatic "To pee or not to pee, that is the question" before heading to the restroom.

The first tip in this chapter should take you a long way in appreciating the nuances of comedic mechanics, and should help you explore situations where you can make people bust a gut at your jokes. Shows, movies and books will also teach you that there are plenty of humourous situations in our everyday lives – it's just that most of us are so busy being "grown-ups" and "mature about stuff" that we've numbed ourselves to the little comedic sub-plots that run through most of our daily schedule – whether on the public transport, in the office or gym, while working, or at home. Comics like Jeff Dunham made their audience crack up by talking about the idiosyncrasies of their pets. It's that simple, and it's something most people can easily relate to – even if they haven't been through that actual experience themselves.

Chapter 4: Some Important Points in Humour

Now that we've discussed how to open you up more and make you funnier, there are a few things you need to keep in mind in you don't want to fall flat on your face.

Audience

As I've mentioned before, your audience could make or break a great joke. It is always vital to keep in mind who is in front of you. While your humour should definitely mirror your own personality and stay true to what you think is funny (unless you're a racist or a chauvinist – in which case, do us a favor), it should also connect to your audience on a personal level - e.g. A rich man cracking a golf club joke in a soup kitchen isn't funny, quite the opposite actually. That man doesn't necessarily have to have been vindictive or too full of himself to do that, he could have just been clueless. Nonetheless, it doesn't change the reaction that it evokes.

Similarly, if you like puns (ugh) and someone you like enjoys them too, by all means go be dorks together.

As I said before, your jokes should depend strongly on your audience.

Timing

This is indubitably the most critical part of humour. Stand-up comedians spend weeks, months and years perfecting the timing in their routine. Timing consists of two parts – length and speed.

Length deals with the time it takes for you to finish the entire comedic comeback or retort. If someone did or said something silly in one sentence and it takes you four before you get to your point – not funny. So, the best funny and witty responses are short and to the point. Advertisers know the value of this, which is why the most humorous ads have brief, witty and catchy punch-lines.

The second point is speed. This basically means "How soon after something happened did you think of and crack your joke?" As I've mentioned before, if you take ages to think of a response, it won't be funny. The goal is to be quick and beat everyone else to the punch. This is why you should cram your subconscious with comedy so that you can draw funny parallels and throw out an observation or a one-liner as soon as something goes down.

Know When to Stop

This is important for anyone who's not up on stage right now. You're not a stand-up comedian. Your intent is to be funny while socializing, and that's a big difference. While it may be amusing at the start to hang out with someone who's cracking jokes all the time, it gets old fast. People who are trying to be comedic all the time cannot be taken in larger doses, so others shun them most of the time till they feel ready for another dose. This is the big-picture way of saying – Be funny in your own time, but humans are more complex than that. So while you shouldn't whine or sulk when you're not trying to be funny, don't constantly stay in "Jester mode" either. People appreciate charm and wit when it's backed up with some serious intellect and depth of character. You don't have to bare your soul to someone, but they shouldn't think that you have the nuanced personality of a clown either.

Keeping long-term effects aside for a moment, the same thing applies to short-term as well. If you've cracked a few good jokes and made everyone laugh, stop and switch the conversation to another light topic that the people around you might enjoy. People will enjoy your company the most if you crack them up *and* show that you don't just spend all your time trawling the internet for funny stuff to say. If it doesn't seem like your jokes in one direction (or about one-direction, for that matter) are being well received, stop and take a break. Spend some more time listening to others and figure out if you may have read them and their tastes wrong. While it *is* possible to 'guess-timate' and classify people into genres where you may be able to start throwing jokes blindly right off the bat with reasonable success, without needing to know them too well, let's remember you're still deep in beginner-dom to be able to do so yet.

Another aspect is understanding how to regulate jokes so you don't overplay them. This doesn't mean cracking the same joke or punch-line more than once, because that's lame and shows a serious lack of creativity. Instead, what I mean is playing the same "principle" or genre of jokes in similar situations too often.

As an example, let's take the funny exclamations scenario which I proposed in Chapter 3 Tip 2. Once in a while in different groups if you bring up such humour, it's funny. But, if you do this every time your partner comes up to chat with you or tell you something – the next line you'll be hearing will be "Listen. We need to talk."

Don't Be Afraid or Apprehensive

The one thing that all funny people share is style and flair. This doesn't mean that they're clad from head to toe in the most expensive or fashionable clothing. It means that if they tank, they do so in style!

Humour is something that will develop inside you. And I know most of you will try to rationalize and think "I'm going to wait till I'm more confident before I start implementing these changes and cracking jokes, so that I can be sure of doing well". I'm sorry but that's not how it works. You need to start pushing yourself from today onward. Whenever you feel like there's an opportunity to crack a joke, grab it. Being afraid is your biggest obstacle, regardless of how many funny shows you go through or great jokes you come up with. Funny people aren't determined by the quality of the jokes they come up with – most people can say the same range of funny stuff. The **only** ones who truly excel at creative joke writing are the professional comedians at the top of their fields, and even in those cases many of them hire professional writers. That should tell you, funny people are decided by *delivery* not quality – otherwise it'd be their writers who'd be up on stage earning the big bucks themselves. So, stop being afraid and go grab the spotlight you want! Carpe Diem!

Listen to Your Instinct

Not the one that *always* tells you something's going to go wrong or that you're not up to the task. Preferably, tear that one out and throw it away – it's an alien parasite leeching off your confidence. But, I mean the quieter one that *sometimes* whispers, this may not be the time for it. If this voice gets slightly bolder and more certain with each comedy show you watch, that's definitely the one I'm talking about.

But, let me point something out. Funny people bring up humour by going *against* expectations. It's when they do things which are the *opposite* of norm that situations become humourous. If you're bound by your inner voice and let it control you so completely that you never go against it, you'll never grow as a person or ever be funny.

The point of an inner voice is to let it guide your actions along better roads, not let it shut you down. If your inner voice is telling you that a joke is too lowbrow in a certain setting, quickly try to think of ways through which you can make the joke more tasteful or high-brow while still maintaining its humour. Or, if your gut feeling tells you that the crowd around you won't enjoy a certain type of joke, veer away from them – you're an intelligent person, you don't have to be tied down with a single genre of humour. The mark of a comedic great is the variety in their toolbox.

Chapter 5: Other Practices to Boost Comic Delivery

The one arena which helps funny people develop their skills the most is public speaking. Since great public speakers need to maintain composure and practice different speech patterns – light, serious, casual, professional, etc. - in front of much larger audiences for this skill-set, it makes handling and amusing smaller groups a cake-walk. It's also a great confidence booster – the biggest asset of a comedian, amateur or professional. If you can't think straight because your mind is too wrapped up in your social anxiety, then it's not helping you to deliver great jokes in time.

So, put yourself in situations which require public speaking proficiency. Even if you aren't great at public speaking, join some comic delivery and public speaking classes in local colleges, universities or hobby centers. At the end of the day, being funny doesn't just depend on how well you remember random pop culture references from the last 30 years, or how much confidence you can project on their own as individual skills, but how well you can bring it all together into one great package.

If you feel – like some people do – that you just weren't born with such gifts, you give yourself too little credit. If you and your genetic line have survived 'til this point, it's because you followed the rules of "survival of the fittest". This means that, somewhere deep inside your head, you have the ability to communicate in an effective manner and separate yourself from the herd as a prospective alpha. If this seems too much like a simplistic "pop psychology" reductionist view of genetic evolution, it's because it is – but that doesn't change the underlying value of my point.

There are several organizations, like ToastMasters, which take on novice members and help them develop their public speaking and observational humour skill-sets. Membership and advancement in any of these organizations would open up your perspective on the importance of these social skills, as well as put you in touch with silver-tongued masters of the spoken arts who would be able to mentor your development as you strive to find and hone your brand of humour in the quest to become a funnier individual.

Conclusion

Humour is a highly subjective field. What may be funny to one person, may be offensive to another. A joke that may do extremely well in one group, may not necessarily be well-received in another. However, always remember not to take yourself too seriously. Don't try to cover up a *faux pas* with awkward silence. If your joke falls flat on its face, turn it around and make it into an opportunity to make fun of your abysmal comedic skills. As long as you can bust out an ironic or self-deprecating grin when you trip up, and are able to laugh at your own shortcomings, people will always give you more chances to be funny.

Never forget that timing in a funny situation is mostly automatic – you won't get enough time to fine-tune your timing unless you're telling a joke from start to finish.

In the interest of variety, don't forget that emphasizing on random parts of a sentence makes for great humour too. Also, "That's what she said" jokes are well-received in a lot of audiences, although they don't necessarily show wit or intellect. Not taking yourself too seriously also means giving yourself the permission to be a child from time to time. An adult life is only enjoyable when the mind enjoying it is as exuberant and curious and excited about little things as a child's.

In the end, the biggest point is always to have fun. This is why you need to figure out your sense of humour through stand-up comedy, sitcoms, books, etc. You will only relax and enjoy yourself if you're *being* yourself. Otherwise, you'll constantly be on guard not to drop the persona you have created for yourself in order to be funnier.

Also, don't mimic other people. It's not funny and it doesn't require wit, intellect or grace – but rather needs you to perfect the art of being as smart as a parrot (well, maybe that's an upgrade for some people). Did I mention I hate puns?

And before we end: an addict's favorite online encyclopedia? WikiBlow.

Finally, I'd like to thank you for purchasing this book! If you enjoyed it or found it helpful, I'd greatly appreciate it if you'd take a moment to leave a review on Amazon. Thank you!

Printed in Great Britain
by Amazon